The Beautiful Poetry of Football Commentary

The Beautiful Poetry of Football Commentary

Charlie Eccleshare

SEVEN DIALS

First published in Great Britain in 2022 by Seven Dials
an imprint of The Orion Publishing Group Ltd
Carmelite House, 50 Victoria Embankment
London EC4Y 0DZ

An Hachette UK Company

1 3 5 7 9 10 8 6 4 2

A CIP catalogue record for this book is
available from the British Library.

ISBN (Hardback) 978 1 3996 0408 6
ISBN (eBook) 978 1 3996 0409 3

Printed in Great Britain by Clays Ltd, Elcograf S.p.A

www.orionbooks.co.uk

For Lizzie and Frankie, who in their different ways will find this equally baffling. And for Mum and Dad, Thomas and Rose for their love, friendship and support.

Contents

⚽ Anatomy   57

⚽ Aesthetics   79

'To say that these men paid their shillings to watch twenty-two hirelings kick a ball is merely to say that a violin is wood and catgut, that *Hamlet* is so much paper and ink.'

J.B. Priestley, *The Good Companions*

'If that had gone in, it would have been a goal.'

David Coleman

Introduction

'Still Martin Tyler for me,' offered one participant in the conversation.

'Where do you stand on Peter Drury?' said another.

'I like him, but that's almost a whole other genre,' replied another. 'Do you know what, I actually think Jonathan Pearce is quite underrated.'

The discussion went on like this for some time, becoming increasingly heated as people realised just how passionately they felt about their favourite football commentators. Various names were thrown about, with their voices, language and the way they have evolved all discussed in microscopic detail.

And while I should add that this conversation took place between me and my colleagues at *The Athletic* and as such is not exactly a representation of wider society, the fact is, commentators matter a huge amount to football fans. Maybe a disproportionate amount.

Perhaps it is because we are trusting them to narrate some of the most significant moments in our lives. If we had someone talking over, say, the birth of our children, we might feel similarly protective. (Frankie, if you ever get to reading this one day, apologies that I'm comparing the moment you entered the world with a Peter Drury monologue).

Either way, football commentators are again and again entrusted with capturing the moment and relaying it to millions of viewers who are hanging on their every word.

And, as this anthology shows, again and again they deliver. Often with a poetic flourish and rhetorical sophistication that would have had some of the great classical orators nodding in appreciation. The Roman writer and politician Cicero, for instance, might have been bewildered by most of what you're about to read, but as a man who knew a thing or two about a tricolon, he would have found plenty of common ground with many of the commentators featured in this book.

Even William Shakespeare would appreciate some of the rhythms and wordplay compiled here. Shakespeare did actually make two references to football in his works, including in Act 2 Scene 1 of *The Comedy of Errors*, when Dromio asks Ephesus: 'Am I so round with you as you with me, / That like a football you do spurn me thus?'

That kind of imagery has worked its way into football commentary, which shares a surprising amount with its classical forebears.

On a personal level, my fascination with football commentary started as soon as I became obsessed with the sport, aged seven. It wasn't a conscious thing, but it's funny looking back and realising how many words and phrases I learned from football commentators. I remember on one occasion at primary school my teacher asking if I could improve on 'sad' as an adjective in a story I'd written. I gave it some thought, and after my mind had wandered to whatever end-of-season review VHS I was watching at the time, I offered some alternatives: 'How about "distraught"? "Forlorn"? Or maybe "disconsolate"?' I suggested. I like the idea of my teacher Sue thinking how precocious I was, when in fact I was simply parroting what I'd heard from Martin Tyler.

At around this time, my interest in football and

commentary led to attempts at imitating what I was hearing. This has been a bit of a recurring theme in my life, but rather than doing so with spoken impressions as came later, at this point I would write my own stories that were based around commentaries on matches in which I was playing professionally, in an imagined future. The level of detail was granular in the extreme, and the matches would often have to be stopped when it turned out one of the opposition players was a long-lost primary school friend of mine, and we would enjoy a warm mid-game embrace.

This book then is, I suppose, my way of saying thank you to football's commentators for all they have given me. By celebrating their magnificence, be it their wordplay or imagery or the cadence of their voice. It's also been a great way to finally put that Latin A Level to good use, by applying a similar level of analysis to the words of those watching football that I once used for ancient set texts. And there the doubters were saying it was a pointless subject! Little did they know it would prove to be an invaluable resource when understanding whether Andy Gray was in fact using chiasmus or asyndeton. Messaging my seventy-one-year-old uncle, a former Latin and Greek teacher, to check on this point is one of the more surreal bits of correspondence I can remember having.

Much of the great football commentary does not need to be intellectualised in this way; many of the best moments are simply a visceral reaction to what is unfolding. But others manage to draw out that instinctive, emotional reaction while also inspiring beautiful, poetic verse.

And that is what this is a celebration of. Those moments when it all comes together and we are left with a memorable accompaniment to what is unfolding before our eyes. Sometimes the commentary almost transcends the action in our collective consciousness.

In so doing, the words stand the test of time – some entries in this book go back more than seventy years. And it has been interesting seeing how commentary has evolved in that time – from the evocative David Coleman to the perfectly-pitched Brian Moore to Barry Davies, who felt that brevity was key to his craft. Andy Gray then brought a boundless enthusiasm to proceedings, and it felt at times like he had a direct line to the players, while Peter Drury has established himself as football's poet laureate.

Everyone quoted in the subsequent pages, and many more besides, has contributed in some way to the canon of football commentary.

So thank you to them all, and to my genius colleague Adam Hurrey, who through the *Football Clichés* podcast has given me a platform to talk about the subject on a twice-weekly basis. And whose superlative (learned that from Tyler) appreciation and understanding of football commentary has been such an inspiration.

So enjoy it, drink it in, I swear you'll never read anything like this ever again.

Legacies

Schoolboys' Own Stuff

Is Gascoigne going to have a crack?
He is, you know . . .
Oh, I say!
Brilliant!
That . . . is schoolboys' own stuff!

Barry Davies

Tottenham 3 Arsenal 1, 14 April 1991, FA Cup semi-final, BBC

One of the greatest moments in arguably football's greatest competition deserves an appropriately great piece of commentary.

Davies certainly provides that, reacting to a wondrous free kick scored by a twenty-three-year-old Paul Gascoigne at the peak of his powers against their loathed north London rivals, who were going for the double.

First of all, Davies builds up the anticipation of the moment by asking the viewer a direct question, which is engaging, and also makes what we're about to see feel both unlikely and just about possible. He then gets two goes at answering it – first when Gascoigne takes on the shot, and then again when the ball flies into the back of the net, adding to the feeling that the majesty of the moment is building all the time.

Davies, a Tottenham supporter, provides a final flourish with a pause in the last sentence between 'That' and 'is' which perfectly conveys the breathlessness of what we're seeing. The antiquated language, even in 1991, of 'schoolboys' own stuff' adds an extra layer of charm and gravitas.

Your boys took a hell of a beating

We are best in the world! We have beaten England!
England, birthplace of giants
Lord Nelson, Lord Beaverbrook, Sir Winston Churchill, Sir
  Anthony Eden, Clement Attlee, Henry Cooper, Lady
  Diana
Vi har slått dem alle sammen, vi har slått dem alle sammen!
  (*We have beaten them all, we have beaten them all!*)
Maggie Thatcher, can you hear me?
Maggie Thatcher . . . your boys took a hell of a beating!
Your boys took a hell of a beating!

Bjørge Lillelien

Norway 2 England 1, 9 September 1981, World Cup qualifier, NRK

Bjørge Lillelien's unconfined joy at Norway beating England is one of football's greatest pieces of commentary, and is charmingly unique.

The invocation of historical examples is a classic rhetorical device to add grandeur to the moment, and Lillelien does it here in a brilliantly idiosyncratic way. National icons like Lord Nelson and Sir Winston Churchill are juxtaposed with the boxer Henry Cooper. One could argue that Lillelien's listing of illustrious British heroes almost feels like an unwitting parody of epic poems such as *The Iliad* and *The Odyssey*, whereby the writer would seek inspiration from a higher source. Here, the higher sources are cited ironically to mock the English.

The final flourish sees Lillelien employ the literary device of apostrophe, where a subject who is not literally present is addressed, or a personified object is addressed, such as Yorick's skull in *Hamlet*. In this case, it's then Prime Minister of the UK Margaret Thatcher – Lillelien uses the diminutive 'Maggie', presumably to add to the insult of what he is telling her. That England, the founders of football, have been beaten by Norway.

This is emphasised by the jubilant repetition (after checking if Thatcher can hear him) of 'Your boys took a hell of a beating! Your boys took a hell of a beating!'

A recurring theme in this anthology is that lines of commentary have become so enmeshed in British sporting culture that updated versions of said commentary have subsequently been used in homage to the original verse. This was the case for Lillelien's commentary in September 2005, when the England cricket team beat Australia to regain the Ashes. And it's nodded to in another entry later in the book.

5

Remember the Name

Gravesen forward
Rooney, instant control.
And he curls it . . .
Oh a brilliant goal! Brilliant goal!
Remember the name! Wayne Rooney

Clive Tyldesley

Everton 2 Arsenal 1, 19 October 2002, Premier League, ITV

This is all about capturing the importance and impudence of a sixteen-year-old Wayne Rooney announcing himself to the world by scoring a spectacular late winner against the champions Arsenal, who were unbeaten in 30 Premier League games.

Tyldesley does this through use of the imperative: directly addressing the audience with an instruction. 'Remember the name', because this is someone who will go down in history as one of the English game's greatest strikers. Tyldesley himself was given this exact instruction by an Everton fan shortly before the match, and the iconic words harken back to the culture of posterity popularised amongst the Romantic poets, in which they would write with a future audience in mind. Over time, Rooney's exploits on the pitch have become all the more venerated, and in the process Tyldesley's words all the more apt.

Not only does the repetition of 'brilliant goal' lead Tyldesley neatly into his famous instruction, it conveys the repeated action that viewers around the world will remember.

Stop Football

It can rarely get better than this for English football
In this season, the most incredible season
The nineteenth of May 2012
FIFA, UEFA, stop football!

Gary Neville

Bayern Munich 1 Chelsea 1, 19 May 2012, Champions League final, Sky Sports

At the end of a memorable first season as a commentator, Gary Neville gets so carried away he makes a bizarre request.

Using apostrophe to directly address two of the sport's governing bodies, Neville issues the imperative: 'FIFA, UEFA, stop football!'

The implication is that the game has peaked with Chelsea's Champions League win and can never be surpassed. Neville even recites the date in full, as if it is the end point for football, after which everything will be packed away and we can all move on to something else.

Thankfully, neither FIFA nor UEFA listened to Neville's command.

And Still Ricky Villa

Villa . . . and still Ricky Villa!
What a fantastic run.
He's scored!
Amazing goal for Ricky Villa!

John Motson

Tottenham 3 Manchester City 2, 14 May 1981, FA Cup final replay, BBC

Motson's language is a lot less ornate than many of the commentators whose work is included here, but he's still capable of delivering hugely evocative lines.

And Still Ricky Villa was the title of Villa's autobiography, and captured the moment of the Argentine's slaloming run that produced one of the greatest goals in FA Cup history.

That it came in a final replay, after he had been substituted in the first game after a poor performance, made it all the more special.

The simplicity of the language works very well in this instance, providing an economical accompaniment to Villa's famous winner. That Motson pronounces the name 'Villiar' is a likeable quirk, and echoes midfielder Ossie Ardiles saying 'Tottingham' in Spurs' FA Cup song 'Ossie's Dream', which was released on the eve of the final.

Motson once told me he'd put this piece of commentary in the top five of his career (before you ask, he doesn't have an order within that top five).

Crazy Gang 1 Culture Club 0

And there it is, the Crazy Gang have beaten the Culture
    Club
Wimbledon have destroyed Liverpool's dreams of the
    double

John Motson

Liverpool 0 Wimbledon 1, 14 May 1988, FA Cup final, BBC

Some find the first line here a little too premeditated, but either way it's a magnificent example of using a contemporary reference to make your point. That somehow Wimbledon's Crazy Gang, the personification of pranks and pugnacity, have beaten English football's aristocrats, Liverpool.

Motson creates an antithesis between the two by giving Liverpool a similar epithet, going with Culture Club, a popular band of the 1980s and a name that is both recognisable and appropriate for Kenny Dalglish's team. The juxtaposition of the two nicknames serves to cleverly create a contrast and convey the scale of Wimbledon's achievement in winning the FA Cup final against the odds.

The alliteration of 'destroyed . . . dreams . . . double' then adds a greater potency to Wimbledon's joy and Liverpool's despair.

Ready Steady Teddy

Gazza's bending free kick,

Sheringham heads it on . . . Sheringham!

It's a second goal

It's double Dutch delight

Gazza went to take the corner and the Dutch weren't
   ready, the defence wasn't steady, and there was good old
   Teddy

And toast tonight with a glass of sherrrrrrrrrrrrrry

England 2 Holland 0. Edwin van der Sar, pick it out of the
   old onion bag

Jonathan Pearce

England 4 Holland 1, 18 June 1996, European Championship, Capital Gold

An utterly extraordinary piece of commentary from Jonathan Pearce's Capital Gold days, when he was given licence to say pretty much whatever he wanted and be as loud and raspy as possible.

Here, as England double their lead in the famous 4–1 victory over Holland at Euro 96, Pearce employs alliteration, in 'double Dutch delight', and rhyme to amplify the bedlam of the moment – 'Ready . . . steady . . . Teddy', which is then followed by the half-rhyme of 'sherry', said with such elongated gusto it lasts a full five seconds.

Peak Pearce finishes off with a jingoistic flurry as he instructs Holland's goalkeeper to 'pick it out of the old onion bag'. A now lesser-spotted idiom that came about because of the goal net's likeness to the bag that onions are sold in.

Late Show

McManaman caught very, very late
That wasn't a bus-ride late, that was a horse-drawn carriage
  late
Get your flaming yellow card out referee and take his name,
  for goodness sake

Jonathan Pearce

England 4 Holland 1, 18 June 1996, European Championship, Capital Gold

Actually, I say peak Pearce – this piece of commentary from the same game was arguably better. When England winger Steve McManaman was caught by a late tackle, Pearce describes the lateness of the challenge with increasing irascibility. I'm not sure it entirely makes sense – are horse-drawn carriages intrinsically later than buses? – but you get his point.

And, again, using apostrophe he directly addresses one of the game's protagonists for emphasis, this time focusing his ire on the referee.

The use of the word 'flaming' is a final reminder that this is from a very different era, when broadcasters were far more liberal with what their commentators were allowed to come out with.

They think it's all over

And here comes Hurst
He's got— Some people are on the pitch
They think it's all over
It is now

Kenneth Wolstenholme

England 4 West Germany 2, 30 July 1966, World Cup, BBC

Undoubtedly, one of the greatest bits of improvisation by a commentator ever uttered into a microphone.

In the World Cup final, with England on the brink of their greatest footballing achievement in the final minute of extra time, Wolstenholme delivers his masterpiece.

As he spots supporters running onto the Wembley grass thinking the game is finished, he is provided with the perfect alley-oop to summarise England's triumph ('They think it's all over'), before Geoff Hurst smashes one in the top corner to make it 4-2, giving him the slam dunk of 'It is now'.

'They think it's all over' was such an emblematic line that it quickly entered football folklore, including spawning a mid-90s satirical sports quiz show of the same name. The phrase also appeared in the band New Order's song for the 1990 World Cup, 'World in Motion', although in that case Wolstenholme re-recorded it with the slightly different words: 'Well, some of the crowd are on the pitch. They think it's all over. Well, it is now.'

The Grand National Goal

Charlton, oh a great goal!
Oh that was a goal good enough to win the league, the cup,
the Charity Shield, the World Cup and even the Grand
National

Kenneth Wolstenholme

Manchester United 3 Tottenham 3, 12 August 1967, Charity Shield, BBC

Building on his World Cup final masterpiece from the year before, Wolstenholme delivers another winning description here.

The genius in this example is the accumulating pace and outlandishness of how good he is claiming Bobby Charlton's goal to be. The first three work really neatly as a trio – the league, the cup, the Charity Shield – since the Charity Shield, now known as the Community Shield, is a match played between the winners of the league and the FA Cup. They set up the slightly outlandish but still believable 'World Cup', before the absurd pay-off of 'even the Grand National'.

Horse racing dates back all the way to the Olympics of Ancient Greece, and has been referred to as the 'Sport of Kings' since the seventeenth century, although the phrase refers to the sport's origin as practice for warfare. By invoking it here with the 'the Grand National', Wolstenholme elevates Charlton's goal to one fit for a king.

Drink It In

Manchester City are still alive here.
Balotelli . . . AGÜEROOOOOOO . . .
I swear, you'll never see anything like this ever again!
So watch it, drink it in.

Martin Tyler

Manchester City 3 QPR 2, 13 May 2012, Premier League, Sky Sports

The crowning moment of Tyler's career and one that is partly defined by what he doesn't say.

Yes, the 'AGÜEROOOOOO' line is what makes the piece of commentary most famous, but much of its power comes from what follows: a delicious elliptical pause that lasts a full nine seconds.

It's an almost superhuman act of restraint from Tyler not to jump in and say something, anything, but to instead take a breath and allow the bedlam taking place at the Etihad Stadium to speak for itself.

Tyler then takes another gamble that works – breaking a convention within commentary circles by saying that what you're seeing can never be repeated.

But he was surely right – a team that hasn't won the title for forty-four years clinching it in the ninety-fourth minute having needed two goals as late as the ninety-second.

The final double imperative suggests that it's best to do as Tyler instructs, and 'watch it, drink it in'.

Heaven

Vardy!
It's eleven! It's heaven for Jamie Vardy!
Hold the back page! Hold the front page!
A Leicester player has smashed the record!

Martin Tyler

Leicester City 1 Manchester United 1, 28 November 2015, Premier League, Sky Sports

The rhyming here is what first and foremost brings Jamie Vardy's achievement to life. He has just become the first player to score in eleven consecutive Premier League matches, taking him to, as Martin Tyler puts it, footballing 'heaven'.

Building on 'Hold the back page!' with 'Hold the front page!' is similarly effective in conveying the scale of achievement – switching from the religious imagery of 'heaven' to the more prosaic, but similarly relatable, world of tabloid newspapers.

The final line leaves us in no doubt about how and why this is so unlikely. 'A Leicester player has smashed the record!'

This was early on in Leicester's title-winning campaign, while they were still largely unfancied, and at the time it seemed crazy for someone from a team normally associated with relegation from the Premier League to be 'smashing' one of the division's most prestigious individual records.

God Bless the Premier League

Harry Kane has blown the league wide open
It's no longer a procession but now a title race . . .
That's why we love our league
God bless the Premier League for days like this

Peter Drury

Manchester City 2 Tottenham 3, 19 February 2022, Premier League, Premier League Productions

In what is essentially an ode to the Premier League, broadcast on what is essentially the League's in-house channel, Drury looks up to the heavens, as his classical forebears so often did, to ask for their blessings.

'God bless the Premier League,' he says, using the rhetorical device of apostrophe. Doing so adds to the weight of his words, emphasising the significance he gives to what we've witnessed.

The antithesis of 'no longer a procession but now a title race' is designed to explain the contrast between where we were at the start of the game compared to the end of it.

Back then, things were one way – now, after Spurs have stunned champions Manchester City 3–2 at the Etihad, they are quite another – Liverpool may have a chance of winning the title after all. Drury's use of 'our league', opting for the possessive adjective in 'our', is a classic rhetorical tool to make the listener believe we somehow own a piece of the object being referred to, in this case the highly sought-after Premier League. It should be said as well that 'our league' has also become the subject of mocking for the implied smugness and the way in which the Premier League likes to celebrate itself.

Wayne, what a player

Nani . . . Rooney!
Oh wonderful.
What a goal, at what a time, in what a place!
What a player!
Wayne Rooney, out of this world.

Peter Drury

Manchester United 2 Manchester City 1, 12 February 2011, Premier League, Premier League Productions

This being Peter Drury, a magical moment calls for a well-placed tricolon. Popularised by legendary orator Cicero in ancient Rome, the tricolon is the grouping of an idea in three parts to give it extra potency. Veni, Vidi, Vici (I came, I saw, I conquered) being one of the most famous classical examples, Druy employs one here with '*What a* goal, at *what a* time, in *what a* place'. The rhythm of which gives the commentator's words greater emphasis and that sense of an increasing realisation of what has occurred. He even adds a fourth – '*What a* player' – to give it greater weight.

Finishing off, Drury leans to great effect on another favoured technique of the commentator – using the language of the otherworldly to describe their seemingly superhuman feats. 'Wayne Rooney, out of this world,' Drury says, as he describes Rooney's overhead kick to win the Manchester derby in the closing stages. Drury's words were indeed apt, as Rooney's breathtaking strike was subsequently voted the best goal in Premier League history.

It's only Ray Parlour

Oh no, he's put him through
Oh it's alright, it's only Ray Parlour
Oh no

Tim Lovejoy

Arsenal 2 Chelsea 0, 4 May 2002, FA Cup final, Sky Sports

A poem so perfectly crafted that it's enough to make one believe in the existence of footballing gods.

This was in the age of Sky Sports Fanzone, when a supporter of each club would commentate on the game, accessible via the red button. For the purposes of this book, Sky Sports Fanzone is ostensibly the equivalent of slam poetry. It lacks structure and coherence and usually you'd give it a wide berth, but occasionally it offers up absolute gold.

For the 2002 FA Cup final, the two teams had a 'celebrity' fan, and Chelsea's was the ubiquitous and let's say 'divisive' *Soccer AM* presenter Tim Lovejoy.

The journey Lovejoy goes on from starting with 'Oh no' to finishing with the same 'Oh no' is known as envelope verse, and shows the narrator going full circle. Here, Lovejoy starts by expressing his fear, but is then quickly reassured by the fact that 'it's only Ray Parlour'. This turns out to be possibly the most hubristic line of football commentary ever uttered. (Hubris was, in Ancient Greece, the act of upsetting the gods through one's pride, and Lovejoy appears to have done something similar to the Olympians' footballing equivalents.)

'Oh no,' he repeats as Parlour scores spectacularly to put Arsenal ahead, and he realises what he's done.

'It's only Ray Parlour' quickly went down in commentary folklore, and formed part of the title of the Arsenal cult hero's autobiography.

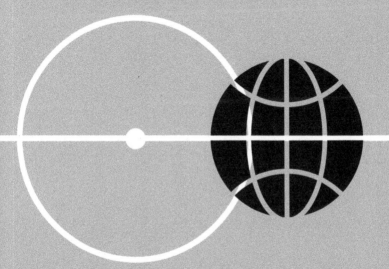

The
Globe

A Worldie from Weir

Lovely footwork there from Weir
Oooh
A special goal in a special game from Caroline Weir
That is world class, that is outstanding
A worldie from Weir

Adam Summerton

Manchester City Women 3 Manchester United Women 0, 12 February 2021, Women's Super League, BT Sport

....

The alliteration in the final line adds gloss to the description of Caroline Weir's spectacular goal. It's a goal so good it drew comparisons with Eric Cantona's famous chip for Manchester United against Sunderland in 1996. The fact that it is scored for City *against* Manchester United makes it even sweeter – especially as the win took Weir's side above their local rivals in the WSL table.

Commentator Adam Summerton earlier employs the repetition of '*A special* goal in *a special* game' and '*That is* world class, *that is* outstanding', with the added alliteration of the g sounds in the former. In the latter example, Summerton also uses asyndeton (replacing 'and' or 'but' with a comma) to give what he is saying more emphasis and make it more concise. 'That is' rather than 'that's', meanwhile, conveys the gravity of the moment.

English Lesson

This is Boniek and he's onside
Two trying to come to him
Surely it must be
Oh what an important foot in by Terry Butcher
But England just cannot afford to make crass errors like
    that
We've got away with it twice, we cannot tempt fate
    further

Barry Davies

England 3 Poland 0, 11 June 1986, World Cup, BBC

We spoke about the footballing gods earlier, and here Barry Davies references them himself – 'we cannot tempt fate further'.

But really this poem is so didactic that the last couple of lines make it sound like an educational pamphlet – a how-to guide on sensible defending. 'Crass errors' is brilliantly schoolmasterly, while the final line is a grave warning about the dangers of pushing one's luck. The repetition of 'cannot' in the last two lines hammers the point home. Gary Lineker's first-half hat-trick was only England's second in a finals tournament, the first being in the 1966 World Cup final. The notion of tempting fate, therefore, is one that would have been at the forefront of Davies's mind.

Italian Lament

They have such talent and they don't take advantage of it
    and make that attacking talent and skill count for them
They were in control of the match and they've lost it
    because they will not learn

Barry Davies

South Korea 2 Italy 1, 18 June 2002, World Cup, BBC

With his final eight words, Davies sums up years of simmering frustration towards one of football's most feted but seemingly fatally flawed nations.

The irritation had actually been building throughout the match, when Italy had scored but typically sat on their lead. The plan backfired as they conceded a late equaliser and then an extra-time 'Golden Goal' to knock them out, prompting Davies to chastise Giovanni Trapattoni's defensive side like naughty children. Just two years previously, the Italians has done the same against France in the final of Euro 2000.

Following the equaliser earlier on in this game, an angry Davies says: 'Three minutes to go and the Italians have been made to pay. Why why do they always do it?'

By the time Italy concede the Golden Goal, Davies' fury has reached even greater heights and the 'will not learn' line comes a couple of minutes after Korea's winner, as if he's still processing what's happened. Swapping 'Italy' for 'the Italians' is common in football commentary, but somehow here it conveys Davies's spitting, seething disappointment, while 'will not' instead of 'won't' adds a formality to proceedings, making Davies sound like a judge delivering a verdict.

The Flip

Again it's Ronald Koeman
Again the problem is there
Again it's a critical moment
He's gonna flip one now
He's gonna flip one
He's gonna flip one
And it's in
  Brian Moore

Holland 2 England 0, 13 October 1993, World Cup qualifier, ITV

One of many lessons football teaches you is that you don't always get what you deserve, and rarely has an injustice been felt as keenly as England's excruciating defeat to Holland that all but confirmed Graham Taylor's hapless team wouldn't be going to the 1994 World Cup.

Ronald Koeman, who narrowly avoided a red card or giving a penalty away for hauling down David Platt as he bore down on goal a few minutes earlier, is standing over a free kick on the edge of the box. Paul Ince sprints out to block the free kick, but Koeman earns another reprieve, after the England midfielder is adjudged to have done so prematurely (in another perceived injustice, Holland had got away with a similar offence from the free kick Platt earned from that Koeman foul).

Moore sets the scene with anaphora – a rhetorical device which repeats the same word at the start of consecutive clauses, in this case 'Again . . . Again . . . Again' – and then, like James Bond realising that the bomb is about to go off, suddenly prophesises what is about to happen. Three times he exclaims that Koeman is 'going to flip one' – a tricolon to foreshadow the tears that Taylor will surely shed.

'And it's in,' he adds after Koeman does indeed flip one into the back of the net and Moore's prophecy comes to pass. A full twenty-two seconds of silence will pass before he begrudgingly concedes: 'An excellent free kick.'

Mad and Crazy

Rahn shoots, goal!
Goal! Goal! Goal!
Goal for Germany!
Germany lead 3–2
Call me mad! Call me crazy!

Herbert Zimmermann

West Germany 3 Hungary 2, 4 July 1954, World Cup final, Nordwestdeutscher Rundfunk

There are a couple of elements that set this poem apart. One is the final line – the imperative to the listener to call the commentator 'mad' and 'crazy'.

That direct communication makes the moment even more vivid, as Herbert Zimmermann reacts incredulously to the magnitude of the moment. This was, after all, the Miracle of Bern, when West Germany came from two down to beat Hungary's Mighty Magyars in the 1954 World Cup final against all the odds.

But that final line is given even greater weight by the eight-second pause that comes before 'Germany lead 3–2'. Bear in mind that this was a radio commentary, and that kind of silence was unheard of, literally.

The repetition of 'Goal! Goal! Goal!' further conveys the frenzied nature of what is happening. We may now think of Germany as powerhouses on the world stage, but this was their first world title and was won against one of the greatest sides of all time, so Zimmermann's enthusiastic entreaty to the listener makes perfect sense.

Lifesaver

Oh, can you believe this?!
Abby Wambach has saved the USA's life in this World
  Cup!

Ian Darke

Brazil 2 USA 2 (3–5 pens), 10 July 2011, Women's World Cup quarter-final, ESPN

The imagery of life and death is not as commonplace as one might think in football commentary. It's especially surprising given we so often think of the sport as a matter of those two states.

Here, though, Ian Darke does use it, and to good effect. With the USA trailing to Brazil in the last minute of extra time in the World Cup quarter-final of 2011, Abby Wambach heads a late, late equaliser from Megan Rapinoe's cross.

'Abby Wambach has saved the USA's life in this World Cup!' Darke says, vividly describing how the forward has essentially resuscitated her team in the tournament.

USA went on to win the match on a penalty shootout, but ultimately lose in the final to Japan.

Miracle of Munich

Beckham, to Scholes again
Now, Heskey's to his left unmarked
Could it be five?
Yes, it is!

John Motson

Germany 1 England 5, 1 September 2001, World Cup qualifier, BBC

What on earth is going on? Sometimes when what is happening is genuinely stretching credulity, there's nothing like a rhetorical question to convey that disbelief.

Motson does exactly that, the classic one-two punch of the question and then the emphatic, exclamatory answer.

Can England really be about to score five goals against the team who almost always find a way of beating them? Can that really be Emile Heskey about to finish with such calmness? It is.

Notably, when Emile Heskey released his autobiography in 2019, it was titled *Even Heskey Scored*, which suggests a level of self-awareness rarely seen in footballers and is perhaps a nod to Motson's incredulity when he scored this goal.

Solid Gold

It's only twelve inches high
Solid gold
And it means England are the world champions

Kenneth Wolstenholme

England 4 West Germany 2, 30 July 1966, World Cup final, BBC

A piece of commentary overshadowed by Wolstenholme's 'they think it's all over' line earlier in the day, this was the one the man himself was much more proud of. It was even played at the funeral of England's World Cup-winning captain, Bobby Moore.

It is a triplet that is all about the physical prize at stake and its symbolism, rather than the feats that have taken England to the point where it's theirs.

The contrast of its small stature with the fact that it's solid gold gets across the fact that the Jules Rimet trophy is both physically unassuming and impressive at the same time.

And it sets up the final line – that whatever the trophy looks like, all that matters is what it represents. That England are 'the world champions'.

Goal for all Africa

It's Tshabalala
Goal Bafana Bafana
Goal for South Africa
Goal for all Africa

Peter Drury

South Africa 1 Mexico 1, 11 June 2010, World Cup, ITV

Always a great appreciator of his surroundings, Peter Drury conveys the importance of a World Cup being held in Africa for the first time.

He does so in typical style, using the tricolon of the final three lines to build up the importance of the moment to a crescendo. Drury also employs anaphora – 'Goal . . . goal for . . . goal for . . .'

It conveys that the impact of Siphiwe Tshabalala's rocket, in the first ever World Cup match played on African soil, resonates beyond South Africa to the whole continent – truly a 'Goal for all Africa'. Using the Zulu nickname for the South African football team and then the English version was also a way of Drury getting across how significant the moment was in uniting the country.

'[The goal] did something for the world that day that politics can never do,' he has said subsequently. 'In that stadium in Johannesburg, the world was unified. It was just a beautiful day for sport and humanity.'

Is this for real?

In by Baines . . . Eto'o
Is this for real? Is. This. For. Real?

Peter Drury

Everton 3 Chelsea 6, 30 August 2014, Premier League, Premier League Productions

One of the finest examples of a commentator asking us to question whether we remain in this realm or have entered another world, and maybe one of the most hyperbolic.

While Samuel Eto'o coming on to score as a substitute with his first touch against former club Chelsea was a big surprise, it probably wasn't enough to make us question our entire existence. Even allowing for the fact Eto'o's goal made the score 4–3 in a thrilling match.

Drury hammers the point home when, after asking the initial question of 'Is this for real?', he repeats each word with what sounds like a full stop in between.

The repeated rhetorical question certainly helps Drury convey his own existential angst at Eto'o's header.

Russian Party

Match point, match point!

Akinfeev saves!
It is Russia's party and the party goes on!
Crank up the music
Charge your glass
This nation is going to dance all night!

Peter Drury

Spain 1 Russia 1 (3–4 pens), 1 July 2018, World Cup round of 16, FIFA TV

Football, in Shakespeare's England, was deemed a lower-class sport. Indeed, in the tragedy of *King Lear*, Kent refers to Oswald as a 'base football player', likening him to a commoner. Meanwhile, tennis was regarded as the sport of kings, and is played by Laertes in *Hamlet* and the French Dauphin in *Henry V*. By adopting the language of tennis – 'Match point, match point!' – to anticipate Russia's impending victory against Spain in the World Cup, Drury is unwittingly elevating the importance of the moment beyond the ordinary. All the world's a stage, and Russia look set to achieve greatness on the biggest one.

When the final Spanish penalty is saved, Drury employs another tricolon to draw the reader back into the world of classical antiquity, as he finishes with a hat-trick of images which invoke Bacchus, the Roman god of wine and pleasure. The double imperative 'Crank up the music / Charge your glass' positions Drury as the conductor of the revels and, perhaps, even the fabled god himself.

Anatomy

Franny's Face

Interesting . . .Very interesting . . .
Look at his face . . . Just look at his face

Barry Davies

Manchester City 1 Derby County 2, 28 December 1974, First Division, BBC

Possibly Davies's most famous piece of commentary. The appeal comes largely from its eccentricity, the arresting strangeness of being asked to look at someone's face.

There's also the repetition in both lines, which gives this short poem such a perfectly formed feel.

The emphasis on 'very' and then the high-pitched, disbelieving squeal of 'face' have given this poem even greater resonance. Never has a player returning to their old club to score the winning goal felt so meaningful.

Davies felt that one of the biggest shifts from his generation of commentators to the next was their economy of words giving way to something more loquacious.

Here, Davies uses just seven separate words to achieve immortality.

Look and Listen

Oh yes, what about that?
What about that?
And look at what it means
Just *listen* to what it means

Barry Davies

Tottenham 3 Aston Villa 1, 30 April 1977, First Division, BBC

Reacting to Chris Jones's vital goal in Spurs' (ultimately unsuccessful) battle to avoid relegation, Davies appeals directly to the viewer's senses.

He implores us to 'look' at the emotion of the moment, before deciding that there is an even more visceral experience to be had. That we should 'listen' to what it means. In poetic terms, Davies is employing synaesthesia, whereby sensations such as sight and smell become intertwined. Like any good orator, Davies is taking full advantage of his surroundings.

This is preceded by the repeated rhetorical question of 'what about that?', which is vague but also successful in describing the chaos of the moment.

Genius

Here's Maradona again – he has Burruchaga to his left, and
Valdano to his left
He doesn't . . . he won't need any of them
You have to say that's magnificent
There is no debate about that goal
That was just pure football genius

Barry Davies

Argentina 2 England 1, 22 June 1986, World Cup quarter-final, BBC

Another lesson that football teaches us is magnanimity, and it's delivered here by the most trusted of teachers, Barry Davies.

Having just scored the infamous 'Hand of God' goal that should never have stood, Diego Maradona scores one of the best goals in football's history after a stunning run through the England defence.

By using the second-person 'you', Davies brings the audience into it, as if we are all being forced to acknowledge this universal truth.

Then the juxtaposition of the modest 'just' with the superlative 'pure football genius' – a nod to how Maradona made the seemingly impossible not only possible but almost inevitable.

Little Eel

Maradona, turns like a little eel
He comes away from trouble, little squat man
Comes inside Butcher, leaves him for dead
Outside Fenwick, leaves him for dead, and puts the ball
    away
And that is why Maradona is the greatest player in the
    world

Bryon Butler

Argentina 2 England 1, 22 June 1986, World Cup quarter-final, BBC Radio

In the BBC radio version of Diego Maradona's famous second goal for Argentina against England, Bryon Butler emphasises the player's physicality. First, he uses the marine imagery of 'like a little eel'. He then repeats 'little' and adds the adjective 'squat', which would probably not pass muster by today's standards.

The repetition of 'leaves him for dead' builds up the excitement, and the 'inside . . . outside' cleverly conveys the slaloming nature of Maradona's run.

The final line is said so matter-of-factly as to avoid hyperbole. It's a bold claim but made without any equivocation, which makes it more impactful and inarguable.

He is the greatest and the goal we've just seen is all the evidence you need.

Naked Newcastle

Heighway, Liverpool showing their party pieces, he wasn't
    offside
Smith, yes!
Keegan's second and Newcastle were undressed!
They were absolutely stripped naked!

David Coleman

Liverpool 3 Newcastle 0, 4 May 1974, FA Cup final, BBC

The idea of being naked, of being undressed, is one of the oldest and strongest-held motifs for how humans express their anxiety. To this day, being naked in public is one of the most common recurring nightmares, and ties into all sorts of insecurities about being exposed, of suffering from imposter syndrome.

Here it is Newcastle whose anxiety dream is playing out in public. They have been battered by Liverpool in the FA Cup final, the most public setting of all – especially at a time when the annual Wembley showpiece was one of very few matches shown live on television and reached a huge audience, as well as the 100,000 there at the ground.

The 'undressed . . . absolutely stripped naked' imagery from David Coleman makes Newcastle's suffering vivid and instantly relatable. He would later follow this up with an utterly wonderful rhyming couplet – 'Keegan two, Heighway one / Liverpool three, Newcastle none'. In Elizabethan theatre, such couplets often signalled the end of a scene, and here they signal the end of Newcastle's hopes of winning the FA Cup.

Goalgasm

He's in, he's in
Fernando Torres
Oooooooooohhhhhhhhhhhhhhhhhhhhhhhhhhhhh
Un-be-lievable

Gary Neville

Barcelona 2 Chelsea 2, 24 April 2012, Champions League semi-final, Sky Sports

In Gary Neville's first season as a commentator, he well and truly made his mark here. It was, and is, a bit incongruous with his quickly established blend of thorough research and incisive analysis, but like a footballer known for his artistry, sometimes you just need to do the commentary equivalent of smashing one in from a few yards out.

Neville's 'Oooooooooohhhhhhhhhhhhhhhhhhhhhhhhh' lasts a full seven seconds, and conveys the improbability not just of Fernando Torres's goal completely against the run of play at the Camp Nou, but also of Chelsea reaching the Champions League final despite looking down and out on a number of occasions.

It also gave rise to a new rhetorical device, one that classicists have confirmed wasn't around in the ancient world: 'goalgasm'.

Cantona's Kung-fu Kick

Cantona is dismissed!
Where can there be a place in the game for a man
    of such extravagant talent, a man of such wicked
    temperament?
A man who has quite rightly been dismissed
A man who has now . . .
Oh my goodness me!
He just kicked . . .
He's punched a fan!

Eric Cantona has jumped in and scissor-kung-fu-kicked a
    fan!
I have never seen as disgraceful an incident as that in all my
    years in football
Eric Cantona should be thrown out of the game for that sort
    of incident
I care not one jot about his supreme talent
He launched himself six feet into the crowd and kung-fu
    kicked a supporter
Who was, without a shadow of doubt, giving him lip

Jonathan Pearce

Crystal Palace 1 Manchester United 1, 25 January 1995, Premier League, Capital Gold

A masterpiece from Pearce, who begins with a rhetorical question to illustrate what a conundrum Cantona is. This is emphasised by the antithesis and repetition of 'such extravagant talent' and 'such wicked temperament', and the tricolon of 'a man . . .' The arresting and archaic 'wicked' is similarly well-chosen.

The rest is a beautiful, building realisation of what is unfolding. 'Kicked' becomes 'punched' becomes 'jumped in and scissor-kung-fu-kicked'.

The rhyme of 'I care not one jot' is another Pearcian flourish, as he hyperbolically reveals the details of Cantona's attack on a Crystal Palace supporter.

Atomic

Are you kidding me?
This man is absolutely mainline to pure footballing magic.
This belongs in a different galaxy altogether than we are
    living in
Absolute astonishing, jaw-dropping genius from Lionel
Watch this hesitation right there
Three players inside the telephone box and he don't care
He emasculates them individually, collectively
He literally . . . disperses his atoms inside of his body on one
    side of this defender and collects them on the other
Magisterial Lionel! Magnifico! Extraordinario!

Ray Hudson

Athletic Bilbao 2 Barcelona 2, 27 April 2013, La Liga, Sirius XM Radio

A hearteningly hyperbolic entry from Ray Hudson, a commentator who brings the freewheeling formlessness of poetry slam to the TV and radio mainstream. Here he is talking about his favourite muse: the great Lionel Messi.

On this occasion, after Messi scores a stunning solo goal having come on as a substitute, Hudson goes into overdrive. After the prerequisite incredulous rhetorical question, he begins with intergalactic imagery: 'a different galaxy altogether', before playing with the old football cliché that a player 'could find space in a phone box'.

The language then becomes more aggressive – Messi 'emasculates' the defenders – before borrowing from the canon of science fiction: 'He literally . . . disperses his atoms'.

Hudson signs off with two Spanish adjectives in a nod to where the match is taking place. It's a whistle-stop tour through different worlds, genres and languages, and it's best to just go along for the ride.

Hubris

If a goal is scored now, I'll eat my hat . . .

Thomas Woodrooffe

Preston North End 1 Huddersfield Town 0, 30 April 1938, FA Cup final, BBC Radio

Among all the polished poems collected here, there should also be room for those where commentators have taken it upon themselves to make predictions that have, let's say, not aged especially well.

Because there is something almost classical in tempting the fates and having them instantly make you look stupid.

Back in 1938, the FA Cup final was commentated on by Lieutenant Commander Thomas Woodrooffe, who had gained notoriety a year earlier with his coverage of a naval fleet review. Woodrooffe did so under the influence of several glasses of port and became something of an overnight celebrity.

Here he was, twelve months later, commentating on the FA Cup final, when with the game goalless as it entered the final minutes of extra time he made his lyrical promise: 'If a goal is scored now, I'll eat my hat.'

Sure enough, Preston were awarded a penalty moments later, which George Mutch converted. Thomas Woodrooffe stuck to his pledge and the next day did eat a hat – though it was made of sponge and marzipan.

Have today's experts learned from Woodrooffe's mistake? Of course not. Just ask former England manager Steve McClaren, who did something similar while watching England lose to Iceland at Euro 2016.

Diegoal

Maradona has the ball, two mark him, Maradona touches
   the ball, the genius of world soccer dashes to the right
   and leaves the third and is going to pass to Burruchaga
It's still Maradona! Genius! Genius! Genius! Ta-ta-ta-ta-ta-
   ta-ta.
Goooooaaaal! Gooooooaaaaal! I want to cry! Dear
   God! Long live soccer! Goooooooaaaaallllllll! Diegoal!
   Maradona! It's enough to make you cry, forgive me.
Maradona, in an unforgettable run, in the play of all time.
Cosmic kite! What planet are you from, to leave in your
   wake so many Englishmen?
So that the whole country is a clenched fist shouting for
   Argentina?
Argentina 2 England 0.
Diegoal! Diegoal! Diego Armando Maradona.
Thank you, God, for soccer, for Maradona, for these tears,
   for this:
Argentina 2 England 0

Victor Hugo Morales

Argentina 2 England 1, 22 June 1986, World Cup quarter-final, Radio Argentina

The Argentinian perspective on this goal is understandably emotional. Only four years earlier, the UK and Argentina had been at war over the Falkland Islands, and the wounds were still raw.

Maradona's first goal in this game – scored only a few minutes before this one – was later dubbed the 'Hand of God', and Víctor Hugo Morales reaches for divine language here to describe his second: 'Dear God! . . . Thank you, God'.

He also calls Maradona a genius four times, including three times in succession, and uses the soaring intergalactic imagery of 'Cosmic kite! What planet are you from, to leave in your wake so many Englishmen?'

This poem is also full of raw emotion – Morales says, 'I want to cry!' 'It's enough to make you cry, forgive me' and invites the whole nation to join him. In so doing, he manages to celebrate both the moment's communal and celestial power – the personal, the national and the religious become one.

The simple wordplay of 'Diegoal' alongside the full name – 'Diego Armando Maradona' – helps to convey the multitudes this 'genius' contains.

Aesthetics

What a Hit

Ooooooh you beauty!
What a hit son, what a hit.

Andy Gray

Liverpool 3 Olympiakos 1, 8 December 2004, Champions League, Sky Sports

Part of Gray's appeal when he was football's leading co-commentator was his enthusiasm and appreciation for attacking football.

With only ten words, Gray becomes all of us at this moment – celebrating the majesty and improbability of the strike. With nine minutes remaining, Liverpool had needed two goals to qualify for the knockout stages of the Champions League. After Neil Mellor had scored in the eighty-first minute, they needed just one.

That was the situation when the ball fell to Steven Gerrard, Liverpool's Roy of the Rovers, on the edge of the box in the eighty-sixth minute. His sensational half-volley is perfectly captured by Gray, with the asyndeton of 'what a hit', where he repeats the words but without any conjunction, and the colloquial 'son', which makes it seem as if he momentarily has a direct line to the goalscorer.

Gerrard himself later said that 'Andy Gray's commentary made the goal even better than it was', illustrating the commentator's power to elevate a moment from the memorable to the unforgettable.

A Winner in All But Name

Look at this, admire a strike of unbelievable quality
Unbelievable, unstoppable, unsaveable
This should win a game

Andy Gray

Chelsea 1 Arsenal 1, 10 December 2006, Premier League, Sky Sports

As he so often does, Gray begins by directly addressing the viewer and exhorting them to savour the moment.

He does his best to capture the outrageousness of Michael Essien's late equaliser with the alliterative tricolon of 'unbelievable, unstoppable, unsaveable'. The tautologous 'unstoppable, unsaveable' serving to emphasise the ferocity of Essien's strike.

Gray finishes with 'This should win a game', as he attempts to put a value on such a spectacular goal.

What a Save

Pelé!
What a save!
Gordon Banks!

David Coleman

Brazil 1 England 0, 7 June 1970, World Cup, BBC

The economy of this poem is what stands out. David Coleman uses only six words and yet artfully describes one of the most famous stops in football history.

The save in question is by England goalkeeper Gordon Banks: to stop Pelé from scoring what looked like a certain headed goal, Banks somehow dived low to his right and diverted the ball up and away from the goal. Pelé was the best player in the world at the time, perhaps the best ever, and would ultimately inspire Brazil to win the tournament.

Somehow, Coleman's language strips that all away and reminds us that at its heart this is simply a battle between two, admittedly extremely talented, men.

Economy was Coleman's commentary calling card, and he delivers it par excellence here.

Fantasy

Thirty seconds remaining
Neymar chips it in
Sergi Roberto – he's done it
Can you believe it?
Oh my goodness me, this is fantasy stuff— land
Pinch yourself, that really happened

Ian Darke

Barcelona 6 Paris Saint-Germain 1, 8 March 2017, Champions League round of 16, BT Sport

Treated with a moment that is genuinely unbelievable, Ian Darke reaches for an old commentary favourite: reassuring the viewer that what they're seeing really is unfolding before their eyes. A descendent of the old 'do not adjust your set' cliché.

It's all that is required in this moment, though, as Sergi Roberto completes an improbable comeback that saw Barcelona score the three goals they needed from the eighty-eighth minute onwards (this one in the ninety-fifth minute) to claim a 6–5 aggregate win to knock Paris Saint-Germain out of the Champions League.

Darke is so invested in what is going on he quickly corrects himself from 'stuff' to 'land' in relation to the 'fantasy' that is taking place.

'Can you believe it?', meanwhile, is so often used we think of it as a cliché, but here it does feel like a legitimate question to be asking.

The Three Rs

It was riveting
It was ruthless
And it was Rivaldo!

John Motson

Brazil 2 Belgium 0, 17 June 2002, World Cup, BBC

A simple but effective alliterative tricolon from John Motson to describe Rivaldo's wonder goal for Brazil against Belgium at the 2002 World Cup. It's an effective trio of lines given extra emphasis by the anaphora of 'it was'.

'Riveting' and 'ruthless' are slightly jarring adjectives to describe a goal but they work in tandem, especially once we have the final flourish of 'it was Rivaldo!'

The alliteration was especially pertinent because all the talk at the tournament was of Brazil's 'three Rs' – Rivaldo, Ronaldinho and Ronaldo – with Motson paying homage in his unique way.

Kanu Believe It

It's Kanu, what's he going to do?
Oh, kan-u believe it?
He's flattened Chelsea!
He's hit a hat-trick at Stamford Bridge

Martin Tyler

Chelsea 2 Arsenal 3, 23 October 1999, Premier League, ESPN

A characteristic bit of wordplay here from Martin Tyler, something that over the years has become his trademark.

It works because what Kanu has done is genuinely unbelievable. A fifteen-minute hat-trick to turn a 2–0 deficit into a 3–2 win for Arsenal away at one of their biggest rivals, Chelsea. 'Kan-u believe it?' indeed.

'What's he going to do?' is also well-chosen language for a player who was notoriously unpredictable, while 'flattened' is oddly evocative in describing Chelsea's collapse.

I think, therefore I play

Neves, time to take a touch, and a second, and then a little
    dink
Oh he's a genius
That's incredible
Rúben Neves
He thinks therefore he plays
And he plays the game in a majestical fashion

Mikey Burrows

Wolverhampton Wanderers 4 Watford 0, 10 March 2022, Premier League, Wolves TV

While Sky Sports' Fanzone feature perhaps stretched the poetic forms of commentary past breaking point, the current proliferation of in-house club channels provide a space for coherent work that still breaks free from the strictures of conventional form and, well, attempts at neutrality.

This is beautifully displayed here, after a sumptuous chip by Rúben Neves for Wolves against Watford, commentator Mikey Burrows reaches for seventeenth-century philosophy.

'He thinks therefore he plays,' is a play on René Descartes' famous 'cogito, ergo sum' dictum – 'I think, therefore I am'.

Italian midfielder Andrea Pirlo first co-opted the Cartesian maxim for football, using it as the title for his very successful 2014 autobiography *I Think Therefore I Play*. Neves was inspired by the book and models his game on Pirlo, pointing to his temple after he scores in tribute.

He does so after this goal, prompting Mikey Burrows to refer to the line, before being so inspired he uses the lesser-spotted adjective 'majestical' to describe Neves's magnificence.

Mere Supernatural

Here is Messi away from two, three, four . . . wonderful
    wonderful wonderful!
How good is he?
A mere supernatural goal from Lionel Messi
He has wriggled and tip-toed his way to the gates to
    Wembley Stadium
He is just brilliant, best player in the world bar none.

Peter Drury

Real Madrid 0 Barcelona 2, 27 April 2011, Champions League semi-final, ITV

Such is Lionel Messi's extraordinary talent that he is a gift for commentators.

Peter Drury cherishes that gift, beginning with the repeated 'wonderful' and then asking the audience a rhetorical question that they too are asking. Then there's the juxtaposition of the ordinary with the extraordinary – 'mere supernatural' 'just brilliant' – in recognition of the ultimate player for making the impossible look easy.

Nodding to the bigger picture and creating a sense of a journey, Drury takes us to 'the gates of Wembley Stadium', where the Champions League final is going to be played.

A final that, thanks to Messi's 'wriggling and tip-toeing', Barcelona will be present for at the expense of their loathed rivals, Real Madrid.

To Die For

Scholes, oh that is divine
Absolutely divine.
What a lovely, lovely goal
And that will do them
Glorious
To die for. To smile about. Just to enjoy.

Peter Drury

Manchester United 3 Panathinaikos 1, 21 November 2000, Champions League, MUTV

The tricolon pay-off is truly spectacular from Peter Drury here. The words he uses actually become less sensational as it goes on, rather than building towards a crescendo, but in so doing he describes the simple pleasure of the goal.

It's a beautiful chip from Paul Scholes that Drury is talking about, and he goes on a journey from saying the goal is 'to die for' to realising that it is actually purer than that and should 'just be enjoyed'. Earlier on in the poem, Drury actually begins by describing the goal in god-like terms as 'divine, absolutely divine'.

In a few lines he takes us with him on a circuitous route that captures the simple genius of Scholes's goal.

Liquid Football

Twat! That was liquid football

Shit, did you see that? He must have a foot like a traction
engine

Gooaaaal

The proof is in the pudding and the pudding in this case is a
football

Oof, eat my goal

The goalie has got football pie all over his shirt

Alan Partridge (played by Steve Coogan)

The parody so painfully accurate it continues to be cherished almost thirty years on.

'Liquid football' and 'foot like a traction engine' are such evocative lines they have become a fully established part of the football lexicon.

The botched imagery of the 'proof is in the pudding . . .' description was even echoed five years later by Peter Drury after Chelsea scored to make it 4–0 away at Galatasaray. 'This is icing on a cake so rich as to be . . . thoroughly, thoroughly palatable for those who've travelled from Chelsea,' an excited Drury said from the commentary booth.

Truly, Alan Partridge's World Cup 1994 preview has become the benchmark for commentators to aspire to/avoid.

Mythology

The greatest comeback since Lazarus

The greatest comeback since Lazarus . . . it's there
The Swiss have rolled
William Tell . . . it doesn't matter. Heidi, the lot of you
You've taken a pasting at the Riverside . . . this has been the
   most magnificent of comebacks
The greatest night the Riverside has ever, ever seen

Ali Brownlee

Middlesbrough 4 FC Basel 1, 6 April 2006, UEFA Cup quarter-final, BBC Radio Tees

Another gem from a local commentator, with all impartiality out of the window.

Trying to contextualise Middlesbrough's amazing comeback against FC Basel in the UEFA Cup, which saw them score the four goals without reply they needed after going 3–0 down on aggregate early on, including a ninetieth-minute winner, local legend Ali Brownlee reaches first for a biblical reference. 'The greatest comeback since Lazarus,' he cries. Lazarus, a friend of Jesus, is brought back to life four days after his death by Jesus in the Gospel of John.

Brownlee soon switches his point of reference and channels his inner 'Maggie Thatcher, your boys took one hell of a beating', as he widens Middlesbrough's victims to not just FC Basel, but all of Switzerland. There's the pun of 'The Swiss have rolled' and the reference to two of the country's most well-known characters – William Tell and Heidi – before Brownlee uses apostrophe to address the whole nation directly, with 'the lot of you' neatly summarising an entire nation's history and culture into two throwaway references.

Finishing off, Brownlee goes beyond even the biblical comparison, cleverly echoing the start of this poem by claiming that 'this has been the most magnificent of comebacks'.

Fathomed from the Foundries

That is it. It's Eindhoven. It's Eindhoven.

Boro have made it.

One of the most glorious nights in the history of football.

We go back to 1876, the Infant Hercules, fathomed out of
the foundries of Teesside,

Mined out of the Eston Hills,

We're roaring all the way to Eindhoven and the UEFA Cup
Final.

It's party, party, party!

Everybody round my house for a parmo!

Ali Brownlee

Middlesbrough 4 Steaua Bucharest 2, 27 April 2006, UEFA Cup semi-final, BBC Radio Tees

As it turned out, Brownlee would witness Middlesbrough pull off an arguably even greater comeback a few weeks later.

Having escaped in the quarter-final against Basel, Boro repeated the trick in the semis, as they once again scored the four unanswered goals they needed to go through, and again completed the comeback in the closing moments.

Brownlee stepped up to the plate, this time limiting his references to the history of the club and the town – starting in 1876 when Middlesbrough FC was founded. He speaks of the Infant Hercules, which is the nickname given to the place by the then chancellor of the exchequer William Gladstone in 1862, a reference to its rapidly expanding industry. Brownlee sticks with the industrial theme and employs the beautiful alliteration of 'fathomed out of the foundries of Teesside'.

He finishes off this gritty and poetic passage with another reference specific to Middlesbrough, inviting his listeners to his home for a parmo, a local delicacy of breaded chicken or pork with cheese.

A year after his death in 2016, Brownlee's words from this poem were written on a mural outside the Riverside Stadium to immortalise them for future generations. At the unveiling, the Mayor of Middlesbrough hailed Brownlee's 'undoubtedly poetic way with words'.

Bronze and Golden

Song . . . Henry

Chance . . . goal . . .

He may be cast in bronze, but he's still capable of producing
    golden moments!

Jon Champion

Arsenal 1 Leeds United 0, 9 January 2012, FA Cup, ESPN

A lovely contrast here between the simplicity of the first two lines and the poetic climax. Champion leaves a six-second pause before uttering the final line, as if he's a striker waiting for the goalkeeper to commit before deciding what he's going to do.

The line is worth waiting for, as Champion succinctly explains the ludicrousness of the situation: that Thierry Henry, who was so good at Arsenal in his first spell at the club that they built a statue of him outside the Emirates Stadium, has returned and scored in his first game back.

'I'd noticed the statue on the way into the ground and it just came out that way in the emotion of the moment,' Champion has since explained. The almost antithetical imagery of 'bronze' and 'golden' is a vivid way of explaining the contrast between what should be possible for this supposed historical figure and what he is actually achieving in the present.

The Holy Grail

He's done it!

The greatest night in the history of Chelsea Football Club!
    European Champions!

They've beaten Bayern in their own backyard!

They've found the holy grail after adventure fraught with
    danger!

And Drogba may never play for Chelsea again, he will never
    be forgotten.

He's immortal at this football club.

Martin Tyler

Bayern Munich 1 Chelsea 1 (3–4 pens), 19 May 2012, Champions League final, Sky Sports

The imagery here is fairly typical, using the well-worn motif of the Holy Grail, an oft-used tool dating back to the Arthurian literature of mediaeval times.

Tyler enlivens what could be a tired cliché by reaching back to those questing narratives, and to Greek epic poetry. He cleverly elevates it through by describing Chelsea's run to Champions League glory as 'adventure fraught with danger'. The imagery is all the stronger because of its sporting truth.

The tricolon in the final line sticks with this imagery, describing the hero of the piece, Didier Drogba, in the elegiac fashion familiar to any reader of classical literature. He is departing, he will never be forgotten, he is immortal.

Homage to Henry

Tyler: Plenty of green grass behind them for Arsenal to
    use
To run the ball into
Like this, like this
Electrifying, electrifying
It's four for the foremost striker
Arsenal's Thierry Henry

Gray: I've seen most things in this league in the last twenty-
    five years
I haven't seen anything like him

Martin Tyler and Andy Gray

Arsenal 5 Leeds United 0, 16 April 2004, Premier League, Sky Sports

This eight-line homage to the legendary Arsenal striker Thierry Henry is the culmination of years of brilliance and is brought to life by Martin Tyler and Andy Gray.

On a night when the still unbeaten Arsenal all but confirmed they would be Premier League champions, Tyler sets the scene by describing how vulnerable Leeds look. Which sets him up neatly for 'like this', repeated for emphasis. Tyler again uses repetition with 'electrifying' and then the wordplay of 'four and foremost' to convey Henry's otherworldly brilliance.

After a three-second pause, Gray enters – cleverly contrasting the enormity of the claim he is making with the reserved, almost offhand way he delivers it. As if to say that Henry has made the extraordinary seem ordinary.

Mountain Climbing

Ronaldo!
They have done it in a hurry
Mountain to climb, they've hit the peak already and it's
    Cristiano Ronaldo by himself
The man's a phenomenon
The club's a phenomenon
There's only one favourite now

Peter Drury

Real Madrid 3 Wolfsburg 0, 12 April 2016, Champions League quarter-final, BT Sport

The idea of a journey is common in the language of football, as is the sense of looking up and attempting to scale new heights.

In this instance, Drury uses the idea of a 'mountain to climb' for Real Madrid, who trailed Wolfsburg 2–0 from the first leg of the Champions League quarter-final. Artfully continuing the analogy, Drury suggests that Cristiano Ronaldo's two early goals mean Real have 'hit the peak already'.

To emphasise the achievement, Drury casually employs antistrophe – the same word at the end of successive lines – and repeats 'phenomenon'. Doing so also conveys how Ronaldo and Real are so intertwined – his significance to the team means they are almost as one.

Roma Rise from their Ruins

Roma have risen from their ruins!
Manolas, the Greek God in Rome!
The unthinkable unfolds before our eyes
This was not meant to happen, this could not happen . . .
    this is happening!

Peter Drury

Roma 3 Barcelona 0, 10 April 2018, Champions League quarter-final, BT Sport

A piece of commentary so lyrical that Drury has been asked many times if he planned it in advance. He did not – explaining that there's no way he could have imagined a scenario whereby Roma so dramatically overturned a 4–1 first-leg deficit to knock out the much-fancied Barcelona in this Champions League quarter-final. And especially not one where the winner was scored in the final minutes by the Greek defender Kostas Manolas, who had registered only five goals during his previous four years with Roma.

In order to convey the improbability of the comeback, Drury takes advantage of his location by alluding to antiquity, which gives an already spectacular moment an even more epic feel . Manolas is apotheosised – elevated to divine status – as 'the Greek God in Rome' and the alliterative line 'Roma have risen from their ruins!' conjures a fleeting image of the Roman Empire restored to its former glory.

The tricolon in the final line makes the payoff more powerful, as does the repetition of 'happen' in all three of the clauses and the emphasis of the penultimate word, as we learn that somehow this is happening.

Reunited

Madeira, Manchester, Madrid, Turin and Manchester
   again
Wreathed in red
Restored to this great gallery of the game
A walking work of art
Vintage
Beyond valuation, beyond forgery or imitation
Eighteen years since that trembling teenager of touch and
   tease, first tiptoed onto this storied stage
Now in his immaculate maturity
CR7 – reunited

Peter Drury

Manchester United 4 Newcastle United 1, 11 September 2021, Premier League, NBC and various others

Possibly Drury's most archetypal entry, coming as it does at the start of a game and so having a more scripted, stylised feel.

It is Cristiano Ronaldo's second debut at Manchester United, and Drury is utilising almost every rhetorical device in his armoury to celebrate the returning hero.

Drury begins by listing the locations of Ronaldo's former clubs to convey how his illustrious career has come full circle, culminating in 'Manchester again'. There is a huge amount of gentle, unobtrusive alliteration – 'wreathed in red . . . that trembling teenager of touch and tease' – alongside the sibilance of 'this storied stage'. The depiction of Ronaldo as 'A walking work of art' and football as a 'great gallery' feels apt given that the art world is synonymous with prizing both aesthetic beauty and, of course, unfathomable wealth. Ronaldo, in Drury's eyes, is exalted 'beyond valuation, beyond forgery or imitation'. He is priceless.

'A walking work of art' is also the exact phrase used to describe the biblical figure of Joseph in the musical *Joseph and the Amazing Technicolor Dreamcoat*. This probably unwitting quotation helps to give the scene a quasi-biblical edge – fitting for the return of the prodigal son.

The half-rhyme of 'valuation . . . imitation' adds greater weight to a tribute that is gathering more and more momentum, before it finishes with the pun of 'reunited'.

Hair-dryer Treatment

As electrifying as a hair dryer thrown into a hot tub, my
  friend!
Absolutely breathtaking
He puts the Haitian voodoo rattle on this one when he
  finishes
Oh, like Betamax, they do not make them like him
  anymore

Ray Hudson

Barcelona 4 Villarreal 0, 25 November 2006, La Liga, GolTV

The language used here and the imagery it conjures up are extraordinary, as the unique Ray Hudson luxuriates in Ronaldinho's spectacular bicycle kick against Villarreal.

Ronaldinho was at the peak of his powers at the time, a one-man force of nature who looked like he was playing exhibition football no matter what was at stake.

This particular goal sees him tee himself up for an overhead kick, and prompt Hudson's 'electrifying' simile. The comparison is extremely arresting, and it's made even more vivid by the colloquial 'my friend!' at the end.

He then uses the device of invoking religion and the spiritual world to convey Ronaldinho's supernatural abilities – 'the Haitian voodoo rattle'. In Western society, vodou has been widely associated with sorcery and witchcraft, which suggests that Hudson is comparing Ronaldinho's abilities with the occult, given how beguiling his abilities appear.

Leaving his questionable grasp of Afro-Haitian symbolism behind, Hudson's imagery moves to 1970s technology, comparing the great Brazilian forward to the now defunct video cassette format Betamax.

Again, it's quite a journey.

Deliverance

Silent to Song

Beautifully pulled down by Bergkamp
Oh what a goal
Dennis Bergkamp has won it for Holland
That was absolutely brilliant
From adversity to triumph for the Dutch
They who were silent are now in song

Barry Davies

Holland 2 Argentina 1, 4 July 1998, World Cup quarter-final, BBC

The most famous English-language commentary of this goal comes from Barry Davies, who captures the moment slightly more lyrically than the emotionally invested Jack van Gelder (see p.136).

The final two lines in particular capture the journey Holland have been on, having had Arthur Numan sent off fourteen minutes earlier and then scoring this spectacular winner in the final seconds.

'From adversity to triumph', and then the sibilance of 'they who were silent are now in song' is a graceful and evocative way to describe the experience of both the Dutch fans and the players.

The alliteration of 'beautifully pulled down by Bergkamp', meanwhile, enables Davies to convey and match the artistry of the Dutchman's spectacular goal.

Up for grabs now

A good ball by Dixon, finding Smith
For Thomas, charging through the midfield
Thomas, it's up for grabs now . . .
Thomas, right at the end
An unbelievable climax to the league season

Brian Moore

Liverpool 0 Arsenal 2, 26 May 1989, First Division, ITV

Thanks in part to the anaphora of Thomas at the start of two, almost three, clauses here, Moore delivers a trio of deservedly famous lines.

'Charging through the midfield', 'it's up for grabs now' and 'right at the end' have all become cherished pieces of commentary, and work so well together. The repeated 'Thomas' groups them together and adds to the building tempo as we reach the crescendo.

Even once the tricolon is over, the beautifully judged five-second pause that follows gives it even greater weight.

Moore avoids hyperbole in his choice of words, but still conveys the improbability of Arsenal defeating Liverpool by the margin of victory needed to steal the title from their rivals with pretty much the last kick of the last game of the season. One of the greatest examples of his generation's economy of words, to which Barry Davies has alluded.

Name on the Trophy

Can Manchester United score? They always score.
Peter Schmeichel is forward.
Beckham . . . in towards Schmeichel . . . it's come for
   Dwight Yorke . . . cleared . . . Giggs with the shot . . .
   Sheringham!
Name. On. The. Trophy.

Clive Tyldesley

Manchester United 2 Bayern Munich 1, 26 May 1999, Champions League final, ITV

As we've seen, many commentators have embarrassed themselves by being too bold with a prediction. Others have bolstered their reputation with their clairvoyance however.

On this occasion, Clive Tyldesley describes how everyone is feeling with the line 'name on the trophy' after Teddy Sheringham's last-minute equaliser for Manchester United against Bayern Munich in the Champions League final.

There's something about the rhythm of it as well – the way he condenses a footballing cliché into just four words and says them all with such precision. That they come after a four-second pause gives each of them even greater emphasis.

The first line here is similarly prophetic. Tyldesley asks himself a question, answers it, and then sees United instantly prove him right.

Promised Land

You have to feel this is their year. Is this their moment?
Beckham, into Sheringham . . . and Solskjær has won it!

Manchester United have reached the promised land!

Clive Tyldesley

Manchester United 2 Bayern Munich 1, 26 May 1999, Champions League final, ITV

Tyldesley's 'name on the trophy' claim was confirmed less than two minutes later, as Ole Gunnar Solskjær completed Manchester United's miraculous comeback with a stoppage-time header.

Emboldened by already being proven right on the United always-scoring point, Tyldesley doubles down by suggesting, 'You have to feel this is their year.' He then repeats the trick of asking a question to set up the moment, and then employs an even longer pause, this one lasting nineteen seconds, to create an almighty build-up to his final line.

And then he invokes the biblical 'promised land'.
A promise, he implies, that was made by United after their last European Cup success thirty-one years previously, and has finally come to pass.

Gol di Grosso

It's Pirlo, Pirlo, Pirlo, still Pirlo, shot . . . with the heel
GOOOOAL! GOOOOAL! GOOOOAL!
Grosso! Grosso! GOOAL! Goal by Grosso!
Goal by Grosso! Goal by Grosso!
One minute left! One minute left!
Goal by Grosso! Goal by Grosso! Goal by Grosso!
Incredible! Incredible!
We're ahead with a minute left!
We're ahead with a minute left!
Goal by Grosso!

Fabio Caressa

Germany 0 Italy 2, 4 July 2006, World Cup semi-final, Sky Italia

As much a song as a poem, the rhythm of this is extraordinary. 'Goal by Grosso!' (*Gol di Grosso* in the original Italian) is the chorus that Fabio Caressa keeps returning to.

It's understandable that Caressa might be a touch over-excited – Italy have just scored a goal deep into extra time of an epic semi-final to knock the hosts Germany out of the World Cup, and the goalscorer Fabio Grosso is himself celebrating in a way that mirrors the tempo and jubilation of the commentator's words.

The hallmark of this commentary is the lack of clever wordplay, crafted metaphors or iconic lines. The undulating vowel sounds and sheer exhaustion and exhilaration in Caressa's voice provide the perfect accompaniment to one of the most famous goals in the history of the World Cup. Four years on from being admonished by Barry Davies, Italy appeared to have learned their lesson.

Arise Sir David

Beckham could raise the roof with a goal here
I don't believe it
David Beckham score the goal to take England all the way
    to the World Cup finals
Give that man a knighthood!

Gary Bloom

England 2 Greece 2, 6 October 2001, World Cup qualifier, FATV

The final line here, coming after a gap of more than five seconds, is wonderful. Both hyperbolic and at the same time articulating what every England fan is thinking.

David Beckham has just scored with a stoppage-time free kick to ensure England are going to the World Cup in Japan and South Korea the following year. In so doing, he has spared the nation's supporters the indignity of missing out, the agony of a month spent watching the tournament wishing they were there.

The line is even more potent now, given that more than two decades on Beckham is still waiting for that knighthood. 'That man' is also a clever way of humanising Beckham – describing the ultimate celebrity, England's captain and demi-god as if he were just any old bloke.

Repayment

The booing of the black players . . .
Is repaid there by Tony Brown

Gerald Sinstadt

Manchester United 3 West Bromwich Albion 5, 30 December 1978, First Division, ITV

At a time when the horrific racism towards black players was largely a taboo subject and one ignored by commentators, Gerald Sinstadt decides to acknowledge what is going on.

And he does so with such perfect timing that no sooner has he described what is happening to Laurie Cunningham than the winger has set up Tony Brown to score. It makes for a perfect retort – even better than whatever words Sinstadt was planning on using to condemn the racist bile.

The West Brom team, led by Cyrille Regis, Laurie Cunningham and Brendon Batson, produced a glorious display of attacking football to beat Manchester United 5–3 at Old Trafford on the day.

It really was the perfect way to shut up and 'repay' the United supporters.

Dennis Bergkamp

Frank de Boer plays the ball, very well
Towards Dennis Bergkamp
Dennis Bergkamp, Dennis Bergkamp
Takes the ball down
Dennis Bergkamp, Dennis Bergkamp, Dennis Bergkamp
Dennis Bergkamp, Dennis Bergkamp
Oaaaahhhh

Jack van Gelder

Holland 2 Argentina 1, 4 July 1998, World Cup quarter-final, Nederlandse Omroep Stichting

One of the first examples of a piece of commentary going viral, this gem started to surface worldwide a few years after Holland's Jack van Gelder uttered these immortal words.

I say immortal words, – he essentially just says someone's name eight times in nine seconds, and yet somehow perfectly conveys the sheer disbelief at the divine goal that Bergkamp has just scored. The holy trinity of the sublime control from Frank de Boer's long pass, the touch inside and then the outside-of-the-boot finish into the roof of the net. On a baking hot day in Marseille, Bergkamp's last-minute goal sent Holland into the World Cup semi-finals at Argentina's expense.

Seemingly out of respect, Van Gelder only ever says Bergkamp's name in full here, and when he realises he surely has to move on and say something else, all he can manage is an orgasmic 'Oaaaahhhh'.

Boom Cheick the Room

It's headed away by Arsenal,
Cheick Tioté!
Oooh! Oooh! Oooh!
Boom, boom
Cheick Cheick the room
What a strike, what a goal, what a comeback, what a
    game
There are no words to describe it!
Cheick Tioté lifts the roof of St James' Park with the most
    sensational strike you will ever see
What a game, what a team, what a moment
It's Arsenal 4 Newcastle United 4
You will never ever see a game quite like this . . .
    unbelievable

Justin Lockwood

Newcastle 4 Arsenal 4, 5 February 2011, Premier League, Real Radio North East

As the entries from the great Ali Brownlee have shown, local radio commentary can often mean less balance, more hyperbole – and there is beauty to be found therein.

In this instance, Justin Lockwood's delirious reaction to Cheick Tioté's magnificent equaliser for Newcastle against Arsenal to turn a 4–0 deficit into a 4–4 draw is justified.

The trio of 'Ooohs!', the rhyming mini-song that is a play on the hit 'Boom! Shake the Room', the tricolon of 'What a game, what a team, what a moment' – it all feels appropriate.

And while the language is consistently superlative and hyperbolic – 'there are no words to describe it' 'the most sensational strike you will ever see' 'you will never ever see a game quite like this . . . unbelievable' – what makes it resonant is that Lockwood does, to an extent, have a point.

The claim that 'you will never ever see a game quite like this . . .' has in part been borne out. This game remains the only time in Premier League history that a team has led by four goals in a game and not gone on to win.

Newcastle's Nightmare

Barnes, Rush, Barnes
Still John Barnes
Collymore closing in!
Liverpool lead in stoppage time
Kevin Keegan hangs his head – he's devastated

Martin Tyler

Liverpool 4 Newcastle 3, 3 April 1996, Premier League, Sky Sports

Still the greatest game Tyler has ever commentated on, according to the man himself, and one that enjoyed an appropriate climax thanks to Stan Collymore's stoppage-time winner.

Liverpool and Kevin Keegan's beautiful but fatally flawed Newcastle were both, unsuccessfully as it turned out, going for the title when they met at Anfield in 1996 for this absolute thriller.

The score was level at 3–3 when John Barnes and Ian Rush exchanged passes. 'Barnes' becomes 'John Barnes' as Tyler captures the swell of excitement that is building around Anfield. And then, like a wave crashing onto the shore, we get 'Collymore closing in!'

And to emphasise the wildly contrasting emotions, the final two lines see Tyler powerfully juxtapose Liverpool's situation with Newcastle's pathetic plight.

Adams' Redemption

Now Bould,
And it's Tony Adams
Put through by Steve Bould
Would you believe it?!
That sums it all up

Martin Tyler

Arsenal 4 Everton 0, 3 May 1998, Premier League, Sky Sports

....

Sometimes a commentator is presented with a narrative so compelling that it's their equivalent of an open goal.

Here, the transformation of 'boring boring Arsenal' into Arsène Wenger's sophisticated attacking team is writ so large that, were it to appear in a work of fiction, you would be saying, 'OK, we get the narrative you are pushing here.'

Tony Adams, once a brutish centre-back fighting alcoholism, is now a Shakespeare-quoting teetotal renaissance man, and rather than clearing the ball away is galloping forward and burying a left-foot volley to confirm Arsenal's first title win of the Premier League era. And the man creating the goal? Adams' centre-back partner of the last decade, Steve Bould, a veteran also synonymous with George Graham's 'boring' team.

As with 'Barnes/John Barnes' in the previous poem, Tyler builds excitement and conveys his surprise at what is going on by building 'Bould' into 'Steve Bould' – *Yes, really, it's Steve Bould clipping a lofted through ball.* He then asks a rhetorical question, a favourite device of commentators – 'Would you believe it?!' – his voice reaching a crescendo as he does so. The aptly named Steve Bould almost touches on nominative determinism – the theory that people are psychologically predisposed to pursuing occupations that evoke their name – for the sheer boldness of his pass to Adams.

The final line perfectly 'sums it all up'.

One, Two, Three

Spurs in full cry here
Lamelaaaaaaaaaaaaaaaaaaa!
One, two, three.

Martin Tyler

Tottenham 3 Manchester United 0, 10 April 2016, Premier League, Sky Sports

A niche entry, but a goal that perfectly illustrated where Mauricio Pochettino's exciting, upwardly mobile Spurs were heading. And one that had Tyler in top form.

After Erik Lamela swept home Danny Rose's pull-back to make it three Spurs' goals between the seventieth and seventy-sixth minutes, Tyler conveys both the importance of the goal and the nature of the Tottenham blitz.

Lamela almost gets the Agüero treatment with 'Lamelaaaaaaaaaaaaaaaaaa!'. Tyler evokes one of his own masterpieces with his cadence and structure, suggesting to the listener that Spurs are on the road to a similar epic achievement – a deliverance from disappointment and despair. In another similarity with that piece of commentary, Tyler leaves a long pause (six seconds this time) before delivering his follow-up line.

'One, two, three' gets across the feeling of a pummelling in a boxing bout – exactly what title-chasing Spurs are dishing out to Manchester United, a team they hadn't beaten at home for fifteen years.

Tyler once told me that the commentary for this goal was helped by the roar of the White Hart Lane crowd. 'It's a bit easier when the home team scores because the noise level of the fans tells you how important something is,' he said. 'This was a proper display and a proper result for a proper manager.'

Take a Bow

Tyler: Four added minutes, and Gerrard . . . ooh . . .
   ooooh
Stunning
When you need someone to stand up and be counted
To pull an absolute rabbit from a hat
Steven Gerrard has just done that
We know the name son

Gray: Take a bow, son.
I mean that, take a bow.
You have been immense.
If anyone ever doubted your value to your side,
You have just blown it away
With the most incredible equaliser that we've seen in a cup
   final.

Martin Tyler and Andy Gray

Liverpool 3 West Ham 3 (3–1 pens), 13 May 2006, FA Cup final, Sky Sports

In this duet from Martin Tyler and Andy Gray, the former sets the scene and almost tees his partner up by addressing Steven Gerrard as 'son' after the Liverpool midfielder points to the name on his shirt as he celebrates his sensational stoppage-time equaliser against West Ham in the FA Cup final.

From there it's all about Gray, who had famously called Gerrard 'son' after a similarly special goal against Olympiakos the previous season. On this occasion, Gray employs the device of apostrophe to address Gerrard directly, something that is very unusual for commentators, who generally speak in the third rather than second person. It creates an intimate feeling, a personal connection between the commentator and the player. It's often the case that commentator's will become synonymous with a catchphrase, and for Gray, 'Take a bow, son' is undoubtedly his most notable – and he reserved it for only the most spectacular goals.

This is very much the case here, with Gray giving thanks to Gerrard for providing us with 'the most incredible equaliser that we've seen in a cup final'.

Hooray for McTominay

Red-letter day, Scott McTominay!
Ederson's day to hide
It's Solskjær's day to look to Paradise and say,
'I've done a double over the neighbours.'

Peter Drury

Manchester United 2 Manchester City 0, 8 March 2020, Premier League, Premier League Productions

To capture Scott McTominay's stoppage-time goal that confirmed Manchester United's win over their neighbours City, Peter Drury uses a range of different techniques – with typical enthusiasm.

First there's the wordplay of 'red-letter day' – referring to the colour of United's shirt while using a well-established idiom. The expression, meaning a day of special significance or opportunity, actually dates back to the classical world, when important days in the Roman calendar would be indicated in red.

Drury also lyrically rhymes the expression with the name of goalscorer McTominay, and repeats 'day' in the subsequent two lines. The repetition of the same word emphasises the differing fortunes between two more of the protagonists: Ederson, who has gifted the goal to McTominay, and the triumphant Manchester United manager Ole Gunnar Solskjær.

Finally, there's the biblical imagery of Solskjær 'looking to Paradise' as the rain pours down on Old Trafford.

Suckered in Paris

McFadden drags it down now, a long way out
Raaaaa what a goal, what a goal, what a goal by
    McFadden
Magic from James McFadden, he's a genius again for
    Scotland
They've been suckered in the Parc des Princes
James McFadden from forty yards into the roof of the net
Pick it out, Landreau
France 0 Scotland 1

Peter Martin

France 0 Scotland 1, 12 September 2007, European Championship qualifier, Radio Clyde

Stunning moments occasionally require commentators to reach for words that have never been used before. Peter Martin's scream of 'Raaaaa' after James McFadden's long-range strike for Scotland against France is one such example.

It really was a genuinely astounding goal, made even more so by the shock result it set up. Martin brings the latter point to the fore with the boxing analogy of France having been 'suckered'. It's the *mot juste* to describe how France look winded by conceding McFadden's strike, which is not quite the 'forty yards' Martin hyperbolically claims (although it is about thirty-five).

Then, speaking more as a fan (this is another example of not totally impartial local commentary), Martin employs apostrophe to directly address the France goalkeeper Mickaël Landreau – instructing him to 'pick it out' of the net.

Acknowledgements

Thank you to Orion for coming up with the original concept for this book, and for asking me to write it.

Thanks especially to my brilliant editor Shyam Kumar, who has brought the whole thing to life and been an invaluable support throughout.

Finally, this book wouldn't have been possible without the wonderful and uplifting work of the commentators that make up this anthology: Adam Summerton, Ali Brownlee, Andy Gray, Barry Davies, Bjørge Lillelien, Brian Moore, Bryon Butler, Clive Tyldesley, David Coleman, Fabio Caressa, Gary Bloom, Gary Neville, Gerald Sinstadt, Herbert Zimmermann, Ian Darke, Jack van Gelder, John Motson, Jon Champion, Jonathan Pearce, Justin Lockwood, Kenneth Wolstenholme, Martin Tyler, Mikey Burrows, Peter Drury, Ray Hudson, Thomas Woodrooffe, Tim Lovejoy, and Víctor Hugo Morales.

Index of Commentators and Matches

Bryon Butler   Argentina 2 England 1, 22 June 1986, World
Cup

Clive Tyldesley   Manchester United 2 Bayern Munich 1, 26
May 1999, Champions League

— Manchester United 2 Bayern Munich 1, 26 May 1999,
Champions League

— Everton 2 Arsenal 1, 19 October 2002, Premier League

David Coleman   Brazil 1 England 0, 7 June 1970, World
Cup

— Liverpool 3 Newcastle 0, 4 May 1974, FA Cup

Fabio Caressa   Germany 0 Italy 2, 4 July 2006, World Cup

Gary Bloom   England 2 Greece 2, 6 October 2001, World
Cup qualifier

Gary Neville   Barcelona 2 Chelsea 2, 24 April 2012,
Champions League

— Bayern Munich 1 Chelsea 1, 19 May 2012, Champions
League

Gerald Sinstadt   Manchester United 3 West Bromwich
Albion 5, 30 December 1978, First Division

Herbert Zimmermann   West Germany 3 Hungary 2, 4
July 1954, World Cup

Ian Darke   Brazil 2 USA 2 (3–5 pens), 10 July 2011,
Women's World Cup

— Barcelona 6 Paris Saint-Germain 1, 8 March 2017,
Champions League

Jack van Gelder   Holland 2 Argentina 1, 4 July 1998, World
Cup

John Motson   Tottenham 3 Manchester City 2, 16 May
1981, FA Cup

— Liverpool 0 Wimbledon 1, 14 May 1988, FA Cup

— Germany 1 England 5, 1 September 2001, World Cup
qualifier

— Brazil 2 Belgium 0, 17 June 2002, World Cup

Jon Champion   Arsenal 1 Leeds United 0, 9 January 2012,
    FA Cup

Jonathan Pearce   Crystal Palace 1 Manchester United 1, 25
    January 1995, Premier League

— England 4 Holland 1, 18 June 1996, European
    Championship

— England 4 Holland 1, 18 June 1996, European
    Championship

Justin Lockwood   Newcastle 4 Arsenal 4, 5 February 2011,
    Premier League

Kenneth Wolstenholme   England 4 West Germany 2, 30
    July 1966, World Cup

— England 4 West Germany 2, 30 July 1966, World Cup

— Manchester United 3 Tottenham 3, 12 August 1967,
    Charity Shield

Martin Tyler   Liverpool 4 Newcastle 3, 3 April 1996,
    Premier League

— Chelsea 2 Arsenal 3, 23 October 1999, Premier League

— Arsenal 4 Everton 0, 3 May 1998, Premier League

— Manchester City 3 QPR 2, 13 May 2012, Premier
    League

— Bayern Munich 1 Chelsea 1 (3–4 pens), 19 May 2012,
    Champions League

— Leicester City 1 Manchester United 1, 28 November
    2015, Premier League

— Tottenham 3 Manchester United 0, 10 April 2016,
    Premier League

Martin Tyler and Andy Gray   Arsenal 5 Leeds United 0,
    16 April 2004, Premier League

— Liverpool 3 West Ham 3 (3–1 pens), 13 May 2006, FA
    Cup

Mikey Burrows   Wolverhampton Wanderers 4 Watford 0,
    10 March 2022, Premier League

Peter Drury   Manchester United 3 Panathinaikos 1, 21 November 2000, Champions League

— South Africa 1 Mexico 1, 11 June 2010, World Cup

— Manchester United 2 Manchester City 1, 12 February 2011, Premier League

— Real Madrid 0 Barcelona 2, 27 April 2011, Champions League

— Everton 3 Chelsea 6, 30 August 2014, Premier League

— Real Madrid 3 Wolfsburg 0, 12 April 2016, Champions League

— Roma 3 Barcelona 0, 10 April 2018, Champions League

— Spain 1 Russia 1 (Russia win 4-3 on penalties), 1 July 2018, World Cup

— Manchester United 2 Manchester City 0, 8 March 2020, Premier League

— Manchester United 4 Newcastle United 1, 11 September 2021, Premier League

— Manchester City 2 Tottenham 3, 19 February 2022, Premier League

Peter Martin   France 0 Scotland 1, 12 September 2007, European Championship qualifier

Ray Hudson   Barcelona 4 Villarreal 0, 25 November 2006, La Liga

— Athletic Bilbao 2 Barcelona 2, 27 April 2013, La Liga

Thomas Woodrooffe   Preston North End 1 Huddersfield Town 0, 30 April 1938, FA Cup

Tim Lovejoy   Arsenal 2 Chelsea 0, 4 May 2002, FA Cup

Víctor Hugo Morales   Argentina 2 England 1, 22 June 1986, World Cup

ORION CREDITS

Seven Dials FC would like to thank everyone at Orion United who worked on the publication of *The Beautiful Poetry of Football Commentary*.

Manager/Editor
Shyam Kumar

Assistant Manager/Copy Editor
Fraser Crichton

Goalkeeper/Proofreader
Francine Brody

Defence/Editorial Management
Jane Hughes
Charlie Panayiotou
Tamara Morriss
Claire Boyle

Creative Wingers/Design
Nick Shah
Joanna Ridley
Helen Ewing

Strikers/Contracts
Anne Goddard

Treasurers/Finance
Nick Gibson
Jasdip Nandra

Kit Managers/Operations
Jo Jacobs
Dan Stevens

Chief Analyst/Marketing
Tom Noble

Club Doctor/Production
Katie Horrocks

Sporting Directors/Sales
Jen Wilson
Victoria Laws
Esther Waters
Frances Doyle
Jack Hallam
Dominic Smith
Deborah Deyong
Lauren Buck
Maggy Park
Megan Smith
Charlotte Clay
Rebecca Cobbold

Scouts/Rights
Susan Howe
Krystyna Kujawinska
Jessica Purdue
Ayesha Kinley
Louise Henderson